The Road through the Hills
and Other Stories

Rod Smith

Richmond READERS

R Richmond READERS

The Road through the Hills

A young man visits a sleepy English village to study its historic church. But before he gets there, he lives through some very strange experiences and becomes part of an old woman's past... *The Road through the Hills* and three other short stories make up this exciting collection of original writing.

....

Rod Smith is a writer and teacher. He is from Oxford, England, but he now lives in Paraguay with his wife and young son. When Rod is not writing, he likes playing the piano or taking long walks in the country.

LEVEL 2

The Road through the Hills

It was August. I was on holiday from university. I was studying architecture in London and I was using my holiday to visit interesting buildings. One of the buildings I wanted to see was a church in the village of Melbury, in the south of England.

I arrived in the centre of Melbury one sunny afternoon. I saw a sign on a wall opposite the bus stop. It said 'Church Street'. 'The church must be somewhere along that street,' I thought. 'Should I go there now?' I looked at my watch. It was two o'clock. I decided to find somewhere to stay first.

The sign on the wall opposite the bus stop said 'Church Street'.

'You can stay here,' said the landlord* of the village pub. His name was Ted Burrows. He was a large man with fair hair and a friendly smile. I thanked him and took my bag up to the room.

Fifteen minutes later I was back in the centre of the village again.

I walked along Church Street but I couldn't see the church. I stopped at a house at the end of the street. There was a woman in the garden. 'Excuse me,' I said.

The woman came to the gate. She was tall, with long grey hair and a thin mouth.

'I'm looking for Melbury Church.' I showed her the book I was carrying - *Beautiful Churches of Southern England*. 'But I think I'm lost.'

'Laurence,' the woman said, softly.

The woman came to the gate. She was tall, with long grey hair and a thin mouth.

Laurence? My name isn't Laurence. It's Jamie. And I had never met this woman before. 'Perhaps Laurence is the name of a street,' I thought. I waited for her to continue.

But she didn't say anything else. She just stood there looking at me with her bright blue eyes. I felt uncomfortable.

'Er, can you help me?' I asked.

The woman smiled. 'Of course,' she said. 'Let's go inside.' She opened the gate and walked towards the house.

I didn't know what to do. 'She doesn't know me. Why is she inviting me into her house? Oh well, maybe she's just being friendly,' I thought. I followed her down the path*.

We walked through the front door and went into a room. It was dark inside the room. I began to feel even more uncomfortable.

'Wait here,' she said. She put on the light and left the room, closing the door behind her.

I looked around in surprise. I was standing in a child's bedroom. Opposite me there was a small bed. There was a desk at the end of the bed with a child's book on it. The room had two windows, one above the bed and one on the wall to my right. There were curtains over the windows. The curtains were closed and they had pictures of animals on them. A large box stood in the middle of the floor. It was full of toys – a train, a boat, a football, a broken aeroplane...

'This woman is too old to have a young child, surely?' I thought.

And then I saw the photograph. It was on the wall to my left. It was a very large photograph. I didn't have to stand any closer to see what was in it. There were no people, only hills, fields and a few trees. At the bottom of the photograph was a white gate. There was a wide path on the other side of the gate. The path continued on through the hills. It looked like a beautiful place but it wasn't a very interesting photograph.

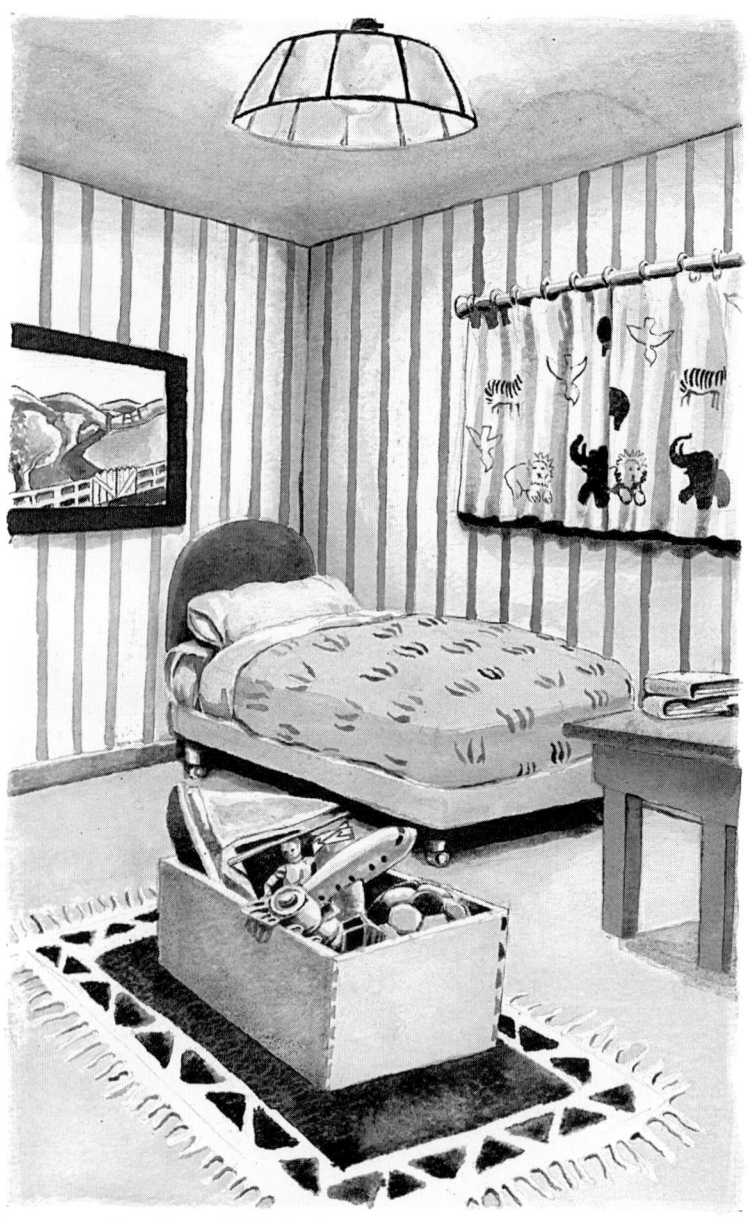

I was standing in a child's bedroom.

'The road through the hills.' It was the woman's voice. I turned around. She was standing behind me. I hadn't heard her come into the room. 'It's such a beautiful place.'

'Er ... yes, it is,' I said. I was surprised. The road through the hills? What did the woman mean? And why was she looking at me in such a strange way?

I decided to talk about something else. 'So, um, where is Melbury Church, exactly?' I asked.

The woman didn't say anything. She just gave me a piece of paper. On it she had drawn a map, a very basic map. It showed a path going to the south of the village. The word 'church' was written at the end of the path.

'I see that the church is to the south of the village,' I said. 'I went in the wrong direction. Your house is to the west.' I smiled at my mistake.

The woman smiled too. 'Come back later,' she said. She took my hand. 'We'll have a cup of tea together. Or two, or three, or four...' She began to laugh.

Now I felt more than uncomfortable. I felt afraid. 'That would be nice,' I said. 'But I must go now. I'll see you later.' I just wanted to get out of the house as quickly as possible.

■ ■ ■

When I got back to the centre of the village, I saw that Church Street didn't continue to the south. 'That's strange,' I thought. 'So why is it called Church Street?' I couldn't think of an answer.

I followed the path on the map. I walked quickly. It was now late afternoon. I wanted to get back to the pub in time for dinner.

I walked for about fifteen minutes. Then I began to feel nervous. The village was behind me now and I couldn't see anything that looked like a church. 'This map is wrong,' I thought. I wasn't surprised. The woman that gave it to me wasn't exactly normal.

Suddenly I noticed that this place was familiar. But how did I know it? I had never been to Melbury before. Then I remembered. The scene around me was the same as in the photograph on the wall in the woman's house – the same trees, the same fields, the same white gate and the same wide path going on through the hills.

There was a noise behind me. I turned around. A man came out of the trees. He had a camera. Before I could ask who he was he took my photograph and ran away.

I didn't follow. I was too surprised. The photographer was wearing a man's clothes. But it wasn't a man at all. I knew who it was. I had seen that face before. It was the face of the woman from the house in Church Street.

■ ■ ■

It was almost seven o'clock when I got back to the pub. Ted, the landlord, was standing behind the bar.

'Good evening, young man,' he said. He picked up a glass. 'You look as though you need a drink.'

'Yes, I do need a drink. A large beer, please.'

Ted looked surprised. 'Is anything wrong?' he asked.

I waited for the drink before I answered. 'I don't know,' I said. I drank some beer. 'But I've just had a very strange experience.'

I told Ted about the woman from Church Street. I told him about her map and described my walk into the country. But I didn't tell him about the person who took my photograph. I couldn't believe it was true. I thought it was just my imagination.

'You are not the first person who couldn't find the church,' Ted said, when I had finished the story. 'It's not to

Before I could ask who he was he took my photograph and ran away.

the west of the village or to the south. It's to the north. People go in the wrong direction because of that street sign. You see, the street isn't called "Church Street" at all. It's called "Churchill Street".' He laughed. 'Someone keeps covering the last three letters. And I think I know who it is. But I don't know why she does it.'

'Do you mean the woman I met this afternoon?'

'Yes,' Ted said. 'Her name is Mary Walgrave. She's lived alone in that house for more than forty years.'

'Alone?' I was surprised. 'But she had a child, didn't she?

11

There's a bedroom in the house, full of toys.'

Ted's expression was serious. 'Yes, she did have a child. A long time ago. She had a son called Laurence. Mary's husband died soon after Laurence was born.'

Laurence? I opened my mouth to speak. But before I could say anything, Ted asked me a question. 'Do you still have Mary Walgrave's map?'

'Yes. Here it is.' I gave Ted the map.

'I thought so,' he said. 'Mary Walgrave sent you to the old railway line*. That place is important to her. Wait here and I'll show you why.'

A railway line? What did Ted mean? I watched him leave the room.

He came back a few minutes later carrying a large book. 'This book will tell you all about Melbury,' he said, 'and about the people that live here, including Mrs Walgrave. I made it myself.' He gave me the book and I opened it.

It was like a historical document. Its pages were full of interesting things about the village – postcards, photographs, old concert tickets...

'Ah yes, here it is,' Ted said. He showed me a piece of paper in the middle of the book.

It was cut from the front page of a newspaper. I looked at the date – 30 August 1958. Below the date there were three words in large black letters – FATAL RAIL ACCIDENT. Below these was a photograph. At first I thought it was the same photograph as the one in Mary Walgrave's house. But it wasn't. The hills, the fields and the trees were the same. But there was no path. In place of the path there was a railway line. The railway line went over the road and there were two white gates on either side of it.

I began to read the text below the photograph.

'And the story doesn't end there,' Ted said, when I had

30 AUGUST 1958

FATAL RAIL ACCIDENT

Mary Walgrave's car after the accident.

YESTERDAY MORNING, a young boy called Laurence Walgrave was killed by a train just outside Melbury. Mary Walgrave, the boy's mother, was hurt in the accident. She is now in hospital. We could not speak to her, but Mr Charles Wells of Melbury, who saw the accident, told our reporter what happened.

'Mary Walgrave loved the sea. During the summer, she often drove down to the coast early in the morning with her young son, Laurence. Sometimes she passed me while I was out walking with my dog.

'Yesterday morning we were walking up on the hills outside the village. I saw Mary's car. It was later than her usual time and she was driving very fast. When she got to the railway line she had to stop. The gates were closed. I saw her get out of the car and look up and down the line. No train was coming.

'Then she did a very stupid thing. She opened the gates and began to drive over the line. She was halfway across when the car stalled*. She got out and tried to push the car to the other side of the line. It was then that I saw the train. I called to her but she could not hear me. I was too far away.

The train came round the corner. It was going very fast. And then Mary saw it, too. But it was too late to do anything. The train hit the car with a great crash. Mary was thrown* to the side of the road. Her son was not so lucky. It was a terrible accident.'

Mary and her son, Laurence, in happier days.

finished reading the article. 'The accident happened at the end of August 1958. The railway company had already planned to close the line in early September. Young Laurence Walgrave was killed by one of the last trains to travel on that line.'

■ ■ ■

The next morning I went to visit the church. I made drawings* and notes. It was a beautiful building. The country around it was beautiful too and in the afternoon I went for a long walk. In the evening I sat in the pub. A man was playing the piano. Everyone sang songs. I stayed up late and had a good time. All these things helped me to forget the sad story of Mary Walgrave and her son.

But the next morning I remembered. I remembered when I opened my wallet to look at my bus ticket and an old photograph fell out. It was a photograph of me as a little boy, standing in the sea. I thought of Laurence Walgrave and felt sad. I also remembered my last words to his mother – 'I'll see you later.' I felt sorry for Mary Walgrave. I decided to go and say goodbye to her.

When I arrived at her house, the front door was open. I went inside.

'Hello?' I called. There was no answer.

I pushed open the door to Laurence's bedroom. It wasn't dark any more. The curtains were open and the room was full of light. But there was only one window, not two. There was no window between the curtains over the bed. There was only a wall with five photographs on it. They were all of the same place – the road through the hills. But this time there was a boy in each photograph. Five different boys. Their faces were different. Their ages were different too. The boy in the first photograph was about eight years old; the one in the second, ten; the one in the third, twelve.

I opened my wallet to look at my bus ticket and an old photograph fell out.

The boy in the fourth photograph was not much younger than me. And the fifth photograph? It wasn't really a boy at all. It was a young man. The young man was me.

At that moment I understood. The photographs told a story. It was a story that began many years ago. It was a story of boys who looked for a church in Church Street in Melbury. Of course, they couldn't find it. When they got to the last house, they asked for help. Mrs Walgrave sent them to a place just outside the village, a place she knew well. When they arrived, she was waiting for them. She took photographs. Then she put the photographs on the wall of her son's bedroom. She looked at them and saw a boy getting older in the place where her real son had died. Other people

16

called that place the old railway line. But she couldn't remember it by that name. The memory* was too sad. So she called it the road through the hills. And then she was happy.

I found Mrs Walgrave in the back garden. She was sitting in a chair, asleep. I didn't want to wake her up, so I decided to leave. And then I remembered something. It was the photograph in my wallet. I took it out, studied it and had an idea.

Mary Walgrave loved the sea. She tried to take her son there one summer's day, forty years ago. An accident stopped her. But could my photograph help her to remember the times she did take Laurence to the sea? Maybe. It could be more important to her than the photographs on his bedroom wall. I hoped so.

I laid the photograph on the chair beside her. I felt better. I was leaving Mary Walgrave with a happier memory. I looked at her for one last time and walked away.

The Music of the Forest

It was a warm evening in September 1951. An American couple★, Larry and June Adams, were sitting on the patio of the Simla Forest Hotel in northern India. There were tall, thin trees around the edge★ of the patio. A line of paper lanterns hung from the trees. By the light of these lanterns a man sat playing the piano. His name was Mr Lal. He was the owner★ of the hotel and he liked to play to his guests★ in the evening. Most of them enjoyed Mr Lal's music.

A line of paper lanterns hung from the trees.

18

But Larry Adams wasn't enjoying the music. In fact, he wasn't enjoying anything very much. And he knew why. Larry was in India because he wanted to kill a tiger. He wanted to hang a tiger's head on the wall of his home in New Jersey. His friend, Ralph, had a puma's head on his wall. But tigers are more dangerous than pumas. Larry wanted to show his friend that he wasn't afraid of dangerous animals. And so he left the hotel every day with his gun* and went into the forest*. But he hadn't seen a single tiger. Now he felt angry and bored, and Mr Lal's strange music was making him nervous.

'What terrible music,' Larry said to his wife. 'Why doesn't he play something we know?'

June smiled. 'We're in India, Larry. You won't get American songs here. Anyway*,' she continued, 'I like his music. It's calm, relaxing and...'

'Strange?' Larry interrupted. 'Because that's what I think it is – strange.'

'I was going to say mysterious,' June said. 'Do you know what your problem is, Larry? You don't have any imagination. You shouldn't kill animals. You should draw* them, like I do. Then it won't matter if you don't find any. You can draw them from your imagination.'

'You're an artist,' Larry said. 'You know how to draw. I don't. But I know how to use a gun.' He stood up and went to the piano.

June picked up her drawing book and followed him.

■ ■ ■

There were empty chairs around the piano. Larry and June sat down. Larry took out a cigarette.

Mr Lal smiled at his guests and continued playing.

'What do you call that music?' Larry asked in a loud voice.

'I wrote this music, Mr Adams. But the inspiration for it comes from the forest. It is the music of the forest.'

Larry looked at June and laughed. 'Maybe that's why I don't see any tigers. They've run away from the music.'

'Don't be offensive, Larry,' June said.

'It is not because of my music that you do not see any tigers, Mr Adams,' Mr Lal said calmly. 'It is because of your gun.'

'The tigers don't know about my gun,' Larry said. 'They are not intelligent enough.'

Mr Lal stopped playing and looked at Larry. 'It is not a question of intelligence, Mr Adams. It is a question of communication. The animals of the forest don't need to see you. They know you are there. And they know you want to hurt them. You must understand that the forest communicates with the animals that live inside it. It is like a mother who guards her children. It tells them of dangerous situations. And the forest can do terrible things to anyone who brings death to it.'

Larry laughed. 'What an absurd idea.'

'I am sorry you do not believe me, Mr Adams. Many men who come here do not believe me. Some of them will never return to their homes. They are dead. And how did they die? They had accidents, Mr Adams. They had accidents in the heart of the forest that no one could explain.'

'I don't believe it,' Larry said. He tried to look calm but June could see that he was nervous.

Mr Lal moved his head closer to Larry's. 'It is true, Mr Adams,' he said softly.

Larry wanted to look away but he couldn't. He was held by the power of Mr Lal's dark brown eyes. He felt their mysterious energy burning into him like red fire. 'Listen, Mr Adams,' Mr Lal said. 'Listen.'

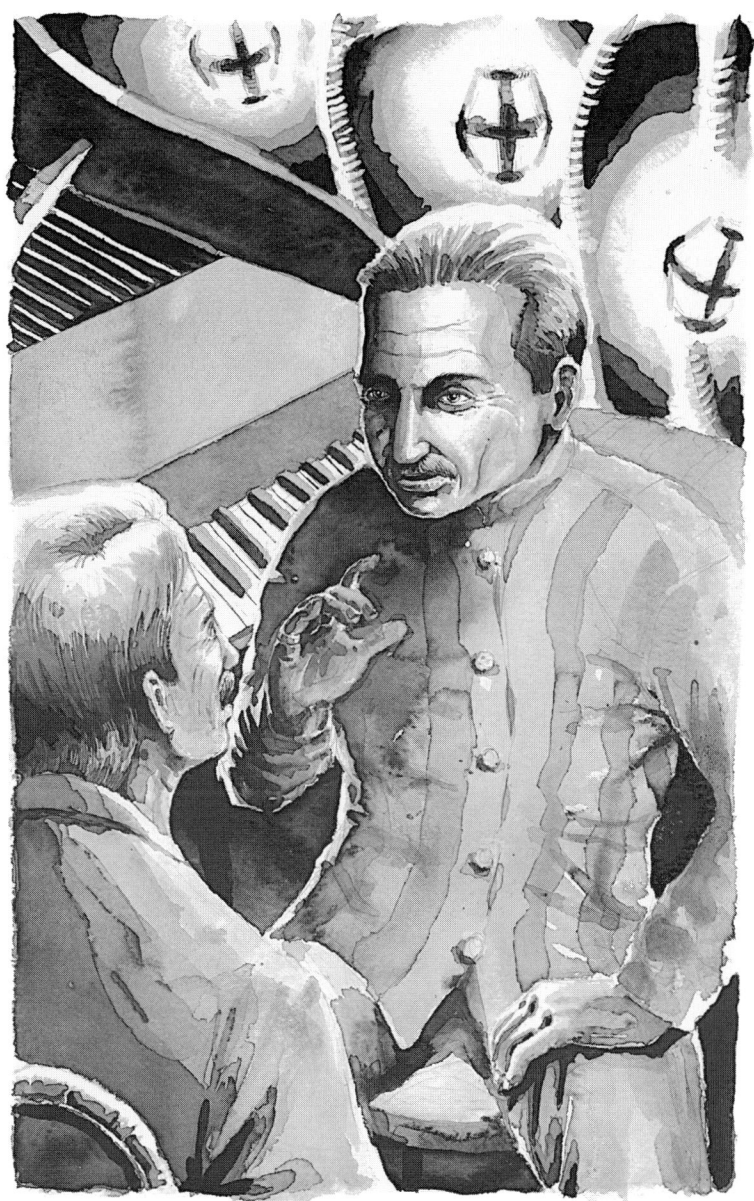

Larry was held by the power of Mr Lal's dark brown eyes.

Larry listened. At first he heard nothing. Then slowly the night sounds of the forest came to him. He didn't like the sounds. They were strange, difficult to identify, and the trees moved above them like an angry sea. He stood up suddenly and spoke to his wife. 'I'm going to bed. I'm bored of Mr Lal's stories.' He turned and walked into the hotel.

June didn't think Larry was bored. She thought he was afraid. She watched him go up the stairs to their room. A noise caught her attention.

It was Mr Lal. He was closing the piano. 'I am sorry about your husband, Mrs Adams,' he said. 'I did not want to make him angry. But I am sad that so many foreign people come here to kill the animals of the forest. I must do what I can to fight for the animals. Maybe that will not be necessary soon. India is an independent country now. I hope the government will stop what is happening.'

'I hope so too,' June said. She saw that Mr Lal was looking at the drawing book in her hand. She felt a little uncomfortable and pushed it to the side of the chair.

Mr Lal smiled. 'I see that you and your husband have completely different interests. He is a hunter*. You are an artist. It is a strange combination.'

'Oh, my husband isn't a bad man, Mr Lal. But he is like a child about some things.'

Mr Lal waited for June to explain.

'Larry has a friend called Ralph,' she continued. 'Ralph is a hunter. He's always talking about the dangerous situations he's been in. I don't believe half of Ralph's stories. But my husband believes them. So now Larry wants to show everyone that he is as good a hunter as Ralph. He thinks he can do that by going home with a tiger's head. That's why he takes his gun into the forest every day.'

'I see,' Mr Lal said. 'And while your husband is looking for animals to kill, you draw them.'

'That's right,' June said.

'Can I see some of your drawings?' Mr Lal asked.

'Of course,' June said. She opened her drawing book and pulled out some of the pages. She gave the pages to Mr Lal. 'I did these earlier today. You can have them. They are a present from me. I would like to show you that I am sorry for my husband's angry words.'

'Thank you,' Mr Lal said. 'But it is not necessary for you to give me these.'

'Please accept them,' June said.

'Very well. And thank you.' Mr Lal held the pages under the light of one of the lanterns. A crowd of forest animals looked back at him. 'These are beautiful, Mrs Adams.'

'I would like my husband to agree with you,' June said. 'I'm always hoping he'll stop hunting and take an interest in other things. But I'm beginning to think that's an impossible dream.'

June saw that Mr Lal was looking at the drawings very closely. When he finally looked up, there was a strange light in his eyes. 'Impossible? Nothing is impossible, Mrs Adams.'

Together they walked into the hotel. Mr Lal stopped at the bottom of the stairs. 'Goodnight, Mrs Adams. Sleep well. Maybe tomorrow will bring better things.' He smiled mysteriously, and left her.

■ ■ ■

June Adams did sleep well that night. But Larry did not. He had terrible dreams. At three o'clock in the morning he woke up. He felt hot and uncomfortable. He looked at his wife. She was sleeping calmly. 'Why can't I sleep like that?' he asked himself. He sat up. Their bedroom was above the

June gave the pages of drawings to Mr Lal.

patio. The window was open and he could hear the sounds of the forest outside. He thought of Mr Lal's words – 'The forest can do terrible things to anyone who brings death to it.' – and he felt afraid.

Suddenly something moved on the wall opposite the window. Larry looked at the wall and saw a crowd of strange black forms. They seemed to dance to the sound of the trees in the soft yellow light that came through the open window.

'What are they?' Larry asked himself. Then he saw that they were shadows – shadows of the animals of the forest. He didn't like the way they moved. He felt they were going to attack him. He closed his eyes. But that didn't help. He imagined the animals pulling him through the window into the dark, singing trees.

He saw that they were shadows - shadows of the animals of the forest.

Larry was very afraid now. He got out of bed and ran to the bathroom. He closed the door. The sounds were quieter and he began to feel better. He also began to think that maybe Mr Lal was right.

■ ■ ■

At nine o'clock the next morning Mrs Adams was standing on the patio with Mr Lal. She was saying goodbye.

'My husband has decided to leave early,' June explained. 'I'm very sorry to go. I have enjoyed being here. But I am happy in another way.'

'In what way, Mrs Adams?' Mr Lal asked.

'Larry told me this morning that he's tired of hunting. He'd like us to visit the Taj Mahal and the Pearl Mosque at Agra. I'm happy because he's beginning to show an interest in other things. I think that is because of you, because of the things you said last night.'

Mr Lal looked up at the lanterns hanging from the trees above his head. 'No, Mrs Adams,' he said. 'It is because of both of us.'

June Adams looked up too. And there, on the outside of each lantern she saw her drawings - one fixed to the outside of each lantern. She imagined their shadows at night, thrown* by the light of the lanterns. 'A very strange and interesting effect, Mrs Adams,' Mr Lal said, with a quiet smile.

The Detective

4

'I'm a detective,' Peter said excitedly, when people asked about his new job. He was young, arrogant and ambitious. He spoke like a private detective in an American film, but he was really English.

Peter was not a private detective. He didn't have an office or a secretary. And he didn't carry a gun* under his jacket. He watched people breaking the law, but he didn't need a gun. The people he watched were not usually dangerous. They were usually poor. They took things from supermarkets. That's where Peter worked – in a supermarket. He was a store* detective. But he called himself a detective. It sounded more important.

■ ■ ■

It was Monday morning, the beginning of the second week of Peter's new job. It was a quiet morning, and not very interesting. Peter watched carefully, but no one tried to take anything. At one o'clock he went for lunch. Exactly one hour later he was back at work.

The first part of the afternoon was as quiet as the morning and by four o'clock Peter was very bored. He decided to go to the music section. It was at the other end of the shop. He knew that young people sometimes went there and tried to steal* CDs or cassettes. He could see it was empty at that moment. But that didn't matter. It was a more interesting place to be and he was tired of looking at food.

Peter began to walk to the other end of the shop. He got halfway and stopped. An old man was standing in the drinks section looking at the wine shelves. It was a warm day but the old man was wearing a long, heavy coat.

'Why is he wearing a coat like that on a day like this?' Peter asked himself. He thought he knew the answer. The old man was going to steal something. He imagined there were large pockets* inside the coat. Perfect places to put things.

Peter didn't want the old man to know he was watching him. He moved to the next aisle* – the fruit and vegetable section – and stood looking at a box of bananas. But he was

An old man was looking at the wine shelves. He was wearing a long, heavy coat.

watching the old man all the time. After a few minutes the old man picked up an expensive bottle of wine and Peter smiled. 'Now,' Peter thought, 'he's going to put the wine inside his coat.'

Suddenly a young woman walked in front of the old man and stopped by one of the shelves. Now Peter couldn't see what the old man was doing. He looked around for somewhere else to stand. There wasn't anywhere. He looked at the girl angrily. And then she took a packet of tea from a shelf and calmly put it in the pocket of her jacket. Peter felt very excited again. 'She's going to steal that packet of tea,' he thought to himself. He forgot all about the old man and went to stand by the main door.

The girl went past the check-out without paying for the tea.

After about five minutes the girl went past the check-out without paying for the tea. She walked towards the exit.

Peter stepped forward. 'Excuse me, young woman,' he said in an important voice. The girl stopped. 'I'd like you to come with me to the manager's* office.'

The girl smiled. 'Why?' she asked. 'Is he going to offer me a job?'

Peter was surprised. Usually people were afraid when he stopped them. This girl seemed calm and relaxed. 'No, he's not going to offer you a job,' he said seriously. 'And this situation is not funny.'

They went to the manager's office. The manager – a short, fat man with a round face – was sitting at his desk. When Peter and the girl walked into the room he stood up.

The girl smiled at him. 'This man said you wanted to offer me a job,' she said.

'I did not,' Peter said angrily. 'I saw this person take a packet of tea from one of the shelves. She put the tea in the pocket of her jacket. Then she tried to walk out of the shop without paying for it.'

The manager looked at the girl and his face became serious. 'Please put everything from your pockets on the desk,' he said.

The girl pulled the packet of tea from her pocket and put it down in front of the manager. She was still smiling.

The manager was surprised. 'Do you agree that you took this tea from a shelf and tried to leave the shop without paying for it?' he asked.

'Of course. I'm not stupid.'

'What do you mean?' the manager asked.

'This tea is mine,' the girl said. 'It's the same as the tea in your supermarket, but I bought this tea on the boat from France last week. Look at the price.' She held up the packet.

'It's in French francs. In the shop on the boat they told me it was duty free*. I wanted to see if that was true. I wanted to compare the price and the size of the packet with one of yours. That's why I put it on the shelf. It was the same size. And it was cheaper. I took it down again and put it in my pocket. I think your...' – she smiled again – ' "detective"... has made a mistake.'

The manager looked at Peter angrily. Peter's face went very red and he looked down at the floor.

The manager turned to the girl. 'I'm very sorry about this. I hope you understand our mistake.'

'Oh, that's okay,' said the girl. She put the tea back in her pocket and left the room.

■ ■ ■

'I think your "detective" has made a mistake.'

Outside the supermarket, a car was waiting. The car was very old and one of its front lights was broken. The girl opened the door and got inside.

'Any problems?' the driver asked. It was the old man with the long coat.

'No, grandfather. How about you?'

The old man laughed. 'No, my girl. No problems at all. That store detective was too busy with you to watch what I was doing.' He opened his coat.

The inside pockets were full of food and drink.

The old man laughed. 'No, my girl. No problems at all.'

The Restaurant

5

Clive Gordon was dreaming of food. He didn't finish the dream. The sound of a telephone woke him up. Automatically, he moved his hand towards the small table by the bed.

'Who is it?' he asked.

'Marcus. I have some news for you.'

Clive sat up. Marcus Baxter was a friend of his. He wrote articles for a local newspaper. He often knew about things before they happened.

'I'm listening,' Clive said.

'An inspector from the *Good Restaurant Guide*⋆ is going to visit your hotel some time today. You should be prepared.'

'Thanks for telling me. But how did you know...?'

'I'll explain later. I must go now. I'm phoning from work.'

Clive thanked his friend and put the phone down.

'Karen,' he called in a loud voice. 'It's time to get up. You've got work to do.'

■ ■ ■

Clive was the owner⋆ of the Flower Garden, a small hotel by the sea. His wife had died several years before and now he lived in the hotel with his fourteen-year-old daughter, Karen. During the summer they were very busy. But winters were quiet. There were very few guests at this time of year, and very little money. Clive wanted to change the situation. He

Clive was the owner of the Flower Garden, a small hotel by the sea.

wanted to make the hotel restaurant famous. 'If I can do that,' he thought, 'people will come here all year.'

There was a good chance that Clive could do this. He was a good cook with good ideas. But he didn't like hard work and his daughter had to do most of the cooking. Every week day, when Karen got home from school, she had to stay in the kitchen until midnight. And she worked all day Saturday and most of Sunday. She hated doing so much work in the kitchen. She never had time to do her school homework or to go out with her friends. She wanted to run away from the hotel. But she couldn't. She had to finish school first.

'Clean those vegetables,' Clive said, when Karen walked

into the kitchen that Saturday morning. 'An inspector from the *Good Restaurant Guide* is coming to eat here this morning. I want everything to be perfect. If he has a good meal, he will put our name in the guide. This is the best chance we have of making this restaurant famous.'

Karen was silent. She thought about all the work she had to do. 'This,' she said to herself, 'is going to be a very long day.'

■ ■ ■

Time passed slowly. Karen's hands were red from washing and cutting vegetables. When she looked at the clock, she saw that it was only twelve-thirty. She felt as if she had been in the kitchen all her life.

Five minutes later her father ran into the room. 'It's the man from the *Good Restaurant Guide*,' he said in an excited voice. 'He's here.'

'How do you know?' Karen asked.

'It's everything about him,' Clive said. 'Well-dressed*, expensive car, important manner. He's also carrying some kind of book. He keeps opening it and writing things down.'

'But couldn't he...?' Karen began.

'Oh, stop asking stupid questions,' Clive said. 'Get the food ready. I'm going to take his order.'

Karen watched her father leave the room. 'Get the food ready yourself,' she said in a low voice.

■ ■ ■

When Clive walked back into the restaurant, there was another customer* in the room. It was a little old woman with grey hair and blue eyes. She was wearing trousers and an anorak. 'She's not important,' Clive said to himself. Her clothes looked cheap and she was carrying a plastic bag.

He thought quickly. The inspector was sitting at a table

She felt as if she had been in the kitchen all her life.

in the middle of the room. He didn't want to put the old woman at a table where the inspector could see her. There was a table beside the door to the kitchen, behind the inspector. She could sit there.

'Good afternoon,' Clive said. 'Follow me, please.' He took the old woman to the table and gave her a menu.

'Thank you,' she said. She looked up to ask for a glass of water. But Clive had gone. He was standing in front of the other customer with a wide smile on his face. The other customer looked important. He was a big man with dark hair and round glasses. He wore a blue jacket with a white shirt and a red tie*. His clothes looked expensive. The old woman listened to their conversation and smiled.

'Would you like to try one of our fine red wines with your meal?' Clive was asking. He put his mouth close to the man's ear. 'The Bordeaux is very good.' He spoke like a man who was telling someone a secret.

The customer closed the wine list. 'It's a little expensive,' he said. 'Maybe one of your "fine glasses of water" would be just as good.'

Clive laughed and put his hand on the man's arm. 'We have special prices today, Mr ... er?'

'Hughes,' the man said. 'Thomas Hughes.'

'Please accept half a bottle of our finest wine at half price, Mr Hughes.'

Mr Hughes was surprised. 'Oh, all right,' he said. 'And thank you.'

'Not at all,' Clive said. 'We like to keep our customers happy.' He stepped back and fell over a chair behind him at the next table. He got up quickly, still smiling. 'Oh, excuse me,' he said.

'What a strange man!' thought Mr Hughes.

Clive went to ask the old woman what she would like to eat.

'Now I can tell you what my name is,' she said, when he came up to the table. 'It's Mrs Williams. And I would like a glass of water to drink and something from your menu. I don't care what you give me. But I want to enjoy it of course.'

'She's trying to be funny,' Clive thought. 'Certainly, Mrs Williams,' he said. He felt uncomfortable and went away quickly.

When Clive walked into the kitchen, Karen was making

Clive stepped back and fell over a chair behind him at the next table.

a Caesar salad. 'Isn't Mr Hughes's meal ready yet?' he shouted.

Karen jumped. 'Who's Mr Hughes?' she asked.

'The inspector. The man from the *Good Restaurant Guide*. The most important customer of the year, you stupid girl,' Clive said angrily. 'Now be quick.'

'All right, all right,' Karen said. 'But be quiet. Someone will hear you.'

Clive's face went very red. 'Don't tell me what to do,' he said. 'The only person who can hear me is you. And you don't listen.'

But Clive was wrong. Someone else did hear him shouting. It was Mrs Williams. She wanted to know what was happening, so she put her ear to the wall and listened to the conversation on the other side. She was surprised. Clive was a lot nicer in the restaurant than he was in the kitchen.

■ ■ ■

More people came to eat. Karen worked very hard. It was difficult. Clive kept going in and out of the kitchen and shouting at her angrily.

At two o'clock, Mr Hughes stood up to go.

Clive walked with him to the door. 'I hope you enjoyed your meal,' he said in a soft voice. 'We are always happy to have you here. Please remember that.'

'Yes, I will,' said Mr Hughes. 'But sadly I don't think I will be here again for a long time. I don't live in this country, you see. I'm just here on holiday.' He held up the book he was carrying. 'Most people take photographs. I like to write about what I see in this little book.'

'But I thought...' Clive began. But Mr Hughes was already walking to his car.

'Excuse me,' said a voice. Clive turned. It was Mrs

Williams. 'I've been waiting for you,' she said. 'I would like to pay for the meal.'

'Er, yes. Of course,' Clive said. There was no enthusiasm in his voice.

'I would also like to tell you,' Mrs Williams continued, 'that I am from the *Good Restaurant Guide*.'

'You! But that's not possible!' Clive said. 'The other man – I thought he…'–

Mrs Williams smiled. 'Things are not always what they

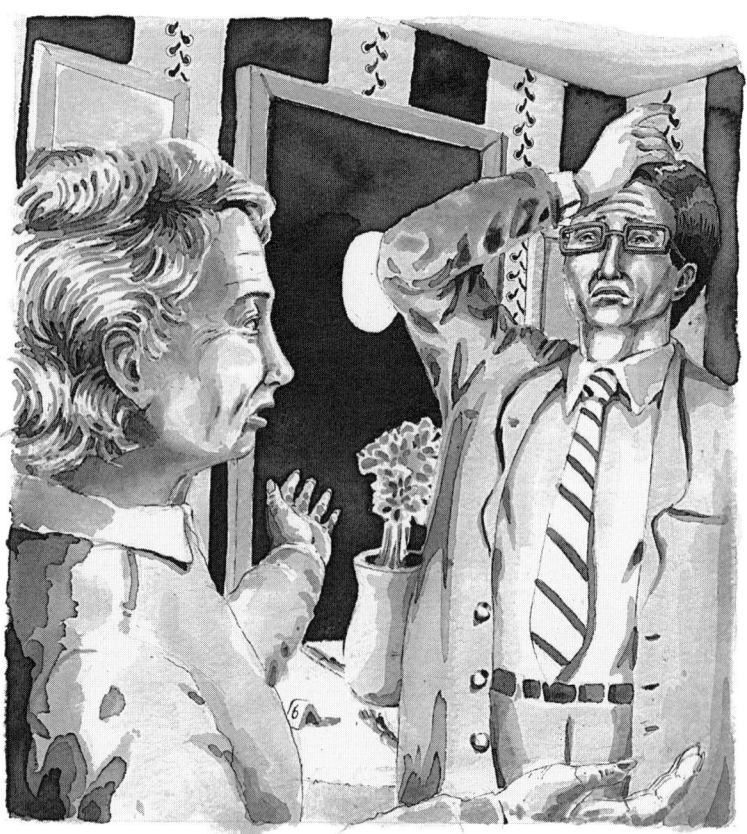

'I don't think I would like to work in your kitchen.'

seem to be, Mr Gordon. Now, about your restaurant. I thought the food here was very good. But good food is not the only important thing for our guide. We need to be sure that the ambience of a place is as good as the food on the table. And the ambience of your restaurant isn't bad. But then there's the kitchen to think about. Oh dear, Mr Gordon. I don't think I would like to work in your kitchen. I wouldn't like to work there at all. For that reason I'm afraid I can't put your restaurant in next year's guide. I'm very sorry.'

Clive Gordon was too surprised to say anything. He watched the old woman walk away. His dream was finished. It was going to be another long winter.

E X E R C I S E S

A Comprehension

The Road through the Hills
Answer these questions.
1 What is the first thing Mary Walgrave says to Jamie and why?
2 Why does Jamie want to leave Mary Walgrave's house 'as soon as possible'?
3 How does Jamie find out who Laurence was?
4 What is different about Laurence's bedroom at the end of the story?
5 Mary Walgrave is sleeping in her garden. Jamie leaves her with a photograph of himself as a little boy. Why does he do that?

Who in the story…
1 …tells Jamie about Mary Walgrave?
2 …saw the 'terrible accident'?
3 …takes Jamie's photograph?
4 …was killed in a car?
5 …sees a photograph of himself on a bedroom wall?

The Music of the Forest
Are these statements true (T) or false (F)?
1 June Adams likes Mr Lal's music.
2 Larry is bored by Mr Lal's stories.
3 Mr Lal thinks June and her husband have the same interests.
4 June wakes up because she can't sleep.
5 Larry decides to stop being a hunter.

Put these sentences in the right order.
1 There were shadows of forest animals on the wall and Larry was afraid.
2 Mr Lal told stories. Larry felt nervous.
3 He got out of bed and went to the bathroom.
4 He left his wife on the patio and went up to their room.
5 At three o'clock in the morning he woke up.

The Detective
Are these sentences true (T) or false (F)?
1 Peter is a private detective.
2 The old man wants to steal things from the supermarket.
3 The manager is angry with Peter.
4 The girl is nervous.
5 The old man is the girl's father.

Answer these questions.
1 What does Peter do after he becomes bored?
2 Why does the girl take the packet of tea from the shelf?
3 Why is Peter surprised when he asks the girl to come to the manager's office?
4 How does the manager know the tea is not from his supermarket?
5 What does the old man do while Peter and the girl are with the manager?

The Restaurant
Answer these questions.
1 Why does Karen want to run away from the hotel?
2 What does Clive do when the old woman walks into the restaurant?
3 How does Mrs Williams know that Clive is unkind to his daughter?
4 Why does Clive think that Mr Hughes is the inspector?
5 What does Clive do when Mr Hughes says the wine is too expensive?

Are these sentences true (T) or false (F)?
1 Karen goes out with her friends every night.
2 Clive doesn't like working in the hotel.
3 Mr Hughes and Mrs Williams are the only customers in the restaurant that day.
4 Clive tells Mr Hughes that he doesn't have to pay for the wine.
5 Mrs Williams thinks the food is very good.

B Working with Language

1 **All these words appear in the stories in this book. Write sentences showing clearly what each word means.**
   forest   well-dressed   memory   drawing   edge
    gun   steal   customer   owner   hunter

2 **Use these words to join the pairs of sentences below:**
   and   because   when   while   but

a I waited. I looked around the room.
b The car stalled. She tried to push it across the line.
c The curtains were open. The room was full of light.
d Other people called it the old railway line. She called it the road through the hills.
e Larry wasn't enjoying himself. He hadn't seen a single tiger.
f June opened her drawing book. She gave some pages of drawings to Mr Lal.
g Larry closed his eyes. That didn't help.
h He saw a girl steal a packet of tea. He forgot about the old man.
i I put the tea on the shelf. I wanted to compare the price and size.
j The man was well-dressed and had an expensive car. Clive thought he was the inspector.

C Activities

1 Imagine you are the driver of the train that killed Laurence Walgrave. Write an account of the accident in your own words.
2 Larry Adams stops hunting and begins to take an interest in other things. June, his wife, is very happy. She knows that Mr Lal has helped to change her husband's attitude. She writes a letter to a friend back in America, explaining the change in Larry. Write her letter.

3 **Either a** The young girl and her grandfather go to a supermarket to steal things. First they make a plan. Write their plan, either as a description or as a dialogue.
Or b When we read *The Detective* we feel sympathy for the young girl and her grandfather. Find sentences that the writer uses in the story to get this response from his readers.
4 **Either a** Karen is telling a friend at school the next day about Mrs Williams's visit. Write their conversation.
Or b Mrs Williams asks to speak in private to the cook at the Flower Garden. She interviews Karen about her life in the kitchen and in general. Write their conversation.
5 What do we use nowadays instead of cassettes? How has technology changed since the time of *The Detective*?

GLOSSARY

aisle *(n)* in a supermarket, an *aisle* is a long corridor with things to buy on both sides

anyway *(adv)* in any case; we use *anyway* when we want to explain, support or make less important what we have just said

couple *(n)* two people who are married, live together or are going out together

customer *(n)* someone who buys something or, here, comes into a restaurant for a meal

draw *(v)* to make a picture with, for example, a pencil; **drawing** *(n)*

duty free *(adj)* you do not have to pay tax on a *duty free* item

edge *(n)* the perimeter

forest *(n)* a large area of trees

guest *(n)* someone who stays in a hotel

guide *(n)* a book which gives you information about something so that you can understand it better

gun *(n)* guns can be used to kill things; revolvers, pistols and rifles are types of *gun*

hunt *(v)* to look for and kill wild animals; **hunter** *(n)*

landlord *(n)* a man who manages* a pub; the pub sometimes belongs to the *landlord*

manager *(n)* a person who controls a business or part of a business, here, the supermarket; a manager always has people working for him/her; **manage** *(v)*

memory *(n)* something you remember from the past

owner *(n)* the person to whom something belongs

path *(n)* outside, a long, thin way on which to walk; there may be a *path* through a garden joining the front door of a house to its gate or there may be a *path* along the edge* of a field where people take their dogs for a walk

pocket *(n)* a place in your clothes to put things

railway line *(n)* parallel metal lines on which trains run

stall *(v)* when a car *stalls*, its engine cuts out and will not start again

steal *(v)* to take something which does not belong to you without permission or, in a supermarket, without paying for it

store *(n)* a shop

tie *(n)* a long, thin piece of material worn with a shirt

throw *(v)* if you *throw* a ball, it flies through the air and then lands; we can use the passive form **to be thrown**: a person might *be thrown* through the air and land on the ground

well-dressed *(adj)* wearing elegant clothes

⬛ Richmond

58 St Aldates
Oxford
OX1 1ST
United Kingdom

Publishing Director: Sarah Thorpe
Managing Editor: Tanya Whatling
Editor: Jane Holt

Cover Illustration: Alison Jay
Illustrations: Alistair Gray
Recording: Maria Jeanette Christiansen, Mauri Corretjé

Printed in Spain
ISBN: 978-84-668-1593-2

© Richmond / Santillana Educación S.L., 2012